SELF CARE GUIDED JOURNAL

MANIFEST YOUR ATTITUDE OF
Gratitude

A DAILY JOURNAL TO PRACTICE POSITIVITY,
REFLECT ON THANKFULNESS AND
CREATE A BALANCED LIFE WITH
AFFIRMATIONS AND DAILY RITUALS

Published by Turtle Publishing
All rights reserved.

Printed on demand in Australia, United States and United Kingdom.

Written & designed by Kathy Shanks
© Kathy Shanks 2021
Illustrations by Freepik Storyset & Turtle Publishing

No part of this publication may be reproduced, stored in a retrieval system, or transmitted in any form or by any means, electronic, mechanical, photocopying, recording or otherwise, without prior written permission of the author.

Under no circumstances will any blame or legal responsibility be held against the publisher, or author, for any damages, reparation, or monetary loss due to the information contained within this book. Either directly or indirectly. You are responsible for your own choices, actions, and results.

Legal Notice: This book is copyright protected. This book is only for personal use. You cannot amend, distribute, sell, use, quote or paraphrase any part, or the content within this book, without the consent of the author or publisher.

Disclaimer: Please note the information contained within this document is for educational and entertainment purposes only. All effort has been executed to present accurate, up to date, and reliable, complete information. No warranties of any kind are declared or implied. Readers acknowledge that the author is not engaging in the rendering of legal, financial, medical or professional advice. The content within this book has been derived from various sources. Please consult a licensed professional before attempting any techniques outlined in this book.

By reading this document, the reader agrees that under no circumstances is the author responsible for any losses, direct or indirect, which are incurred as a result of the use of the information contained within this document, including, but not limited to — errors, omissions, or inaccuracies.

SPECIAL BONUS
FREE BOOKS

FREE Workbook to help you understand the journaling process used in this book.

FREE 30 Days to Greater Self Love Program to follow whilst journaling.

Get FREE unlimited access to these AND all of my new books by joining our fan base!

SCAN WITH YOUR CAMERA OR GO TO
bit.ly/GuidedJournalingWorkbook

Read the book first!

The principles in this Journal are discussed in further details in the book **Guided Journaling** by Kathy Shanks.

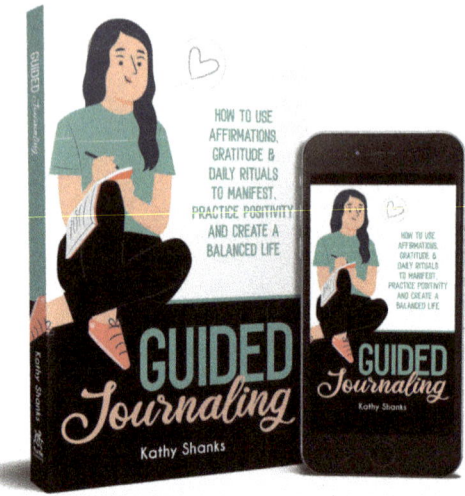

Guided Journaling is available worldwide as print or ebook at Amazon, Booktopia, Barnes & Noble and all good bookstores.

Also available in Australia from **turtlepublishing.com.au**

Inside this book you'll discover how to use my method of journaling to:

- Work towards creating balance for heart, mind, body and soul without sacrificing career and relationships
- Create rituals that help you develop gratitude
- Use daily affirmations to practice positivity and manifest your future dreams
- Discover strategies to improve your relationships, build your life mission, start a side hustle, discover yourself, develop self-love, improve your health AND improve your mindset

It seems too good to be true, right! Organising your thoughts and dreams in 10-20 minutes a day can be that one simple change that actually makes your dreams become a reality.

Make your journal your safe haven, a place of nurturing for you to come and reflect, clear your mind, set goals, develop gratitude, make plans, dream, and take steps towards the future that has always seemed just out of reach.

Please join our journaling community at
facebook.com/groups/kathyshanks
for exclusive insider access to updates and releases

HEART
HEALTH
MIND
RELATIONSHIPS
MISSION

MANIFEST what you want by making a decision

REFLECT
Where are you now?

DREAM
What do you really want?

BRIDGE THE GAP
What are you missing?

DECIDE
What are you going to do?

EXPRESS GRATITUDE for what you have now

EXPRESS GRATITUDE for what the future brings

MANIFEST what you really want

EXPRESS GRATITUDE for the process of change

Create AFFIRMATIONS to support who you need to become

EXPRESS GRATITUDE for results you expect

Create AFFIRMATIONS to support your goals

HEART
Journaling
Affirmations
Meditation
Yoga
Self Love
Gratitude
Earthing
Reading

HEALTH
Journaling
Affirmations
Exercise
Nutrition
Water
Sleep Patterns
Breathing
Rest & Recovery

MIND
Journaling
Affirmations
Reading
Audiobooks
Courses
Education
Ted Talks
Podcasts

RELATIONSHIPS
Journaling
Affirmations
Phone Calls
Dates
Games Nights
Girls Nights
BBQs
Holidays

MISSION
Journaling
Affirmations
Vision Board
Contribution Projects
Planning
Manifesting
Goal Setting
Learning

Focusing on the Heart

What makes my heart full? Am I taking time for myself?
What makes my heart feel light, happy and content?
Let's take the time to reflect, dream, bridge the gap and decide.

ACTIVITY IDEAS: MEDITATION, GRATITUDE, I AM STATEMENTS, AFFIRMATIONS, MUSIC, MOTIVATIONAL BOOKS, EARTHING, JOURNALING, YOGA

 **REFLECT**

Where is my heart now? How do I feel emotionally? What is weighing down my heart, and what is making my heart full?

 **DREAM**

How do I want to feel? What positive emotions do I want to encourage? What negative emotions do I want to overcome?

 BRIDGE THE GAP

How can I bridge the gap between where I am and where I want to be? What activities, methods or tools could help?

 DECIDE

Decide what activities, methods or tools I will commit to. How will I use my journal to improve my daily rituals?

Write it down!
Space for your thoughts.

Affirmations for my Heart

Health Habits

How do I feel about my physical health? Consider how I manage my food, exercise, hydration, sleep, motivation and rest.
Let's take the time to reflect, dream, bridge the gap and decide.

ACTIVITY IDEAS: DAILY EXERCISE, YOGA, WATER REMINDERS, NUTRITION PLAN, SLEEP ROUTINES, BREATHING EXERCISES, TIME IN SUNSHINE

 ## REFLECT

How do I feel about my health at the moment? How do I feel day-to-day? Consider my weight, exercise, sleep, food and water.

 ## DREAM

What is my **ultimate** health goal? Is there something new I'd like to accomplish? How would I like to feel day-to-day?

 ## BRIDGE THE GAP

How can I bridge the gap between where I am and where I want to be? What activities, methods or tools could help?

 ## DECIDE

Decide what activities, methods or tools I will commit to. How will I use my journal to improve my daily rituals?

Write it down!
Space for your thoughts.

Affirmations for my Health

Feed your Mind

What am I doing to nurture and grow my mind? What personal development and education would I like to pursue?
Let's take the time to reflect, dream, bridge the gap and decide.

ACTIVITY IDEAS: LECTURES, TED TALKS, PODCASTS, AUDIOBOOKS, READING, FOLLOW INSPIRING ROLE MODELS, ACADEMIC COURSES

 ## REFLECT

Where is my mind now? How do I feel about what I know? Are there certain circumstances where I feel I lack knowledge?

 ## DREAM

What would I like to learn? Any specific personal development I'd like to do? What knowledge could assist with my career or life mission?

 ## BRIDGE THE GAP

How can I bridge the gap between where I am and where I want to be? What activities, methods or tools could help?

 ## DECIDE

Decide what activities, methods or tools I will commit to. How will I use my journal to improve my daily rituals?

Write it down!
Space for your thoughts.

Affirmations for my Mind

Relationship Status

What am I doing to nurture or build my relationships? Consider my romantic partner, friends, immediate & extended family and colleagues. Let's take the time to reflect, dream, bridge the gap and decide.

ACTIVITY IDEAS: PARTNER DATES, PHONE CALLS, GIRLS' NIGHT OUT, GAMES NIGHTS, BBQS, VISITING ELDERLY RELATIVES, FAMILY HOLIDAYS

REFLECT

How do I feel about my current relationships? Do some need work? Do some cause conflict in my life? Do they rank high in my priorities?

DREAM

What kind of person do I want to be in each relationship? How do I wish some relationships were different? How much time can I give them?

BRIDGE THE GAP

How can I bridge the gap between where I am and where I want to be? What activities, methods or tools could help?

DECIDE

Decide what activities, methods or tools I will commit to. How will I use my journal to improve my daily rituals?

Write it down!
Space for your thoughts.

Affirmations for my Relationships

_____
_____
_____
_____
_____
_____
_____
_____
_____
_____
_____

Life Mission

What am I doing to work on my life purpose? Consider my career, financial goals, business plans and charitable ambitions.
Let's take the time to reflect, dream, bridge the gap and decide.

ACTIVITY IDEAS: VISION BOARDS, SETTING & REMINDING YOURSELF OF YOUR GOALS, PLANNING CONTRIBUTION PROJECTS, MANIFESTING

 REFLECT

 DREAM

How do I feel about where I currently am? Does my current life financially reflect my future goals? Am I managing my time well?

What're my wildest dreams? Do I want to change careers, start a business or reach the pinnacle of my company? How do I want to give back?

 BRIDGE THE GAP

 DECIDE

How can I bridge the gap between where I am and where I want to be? What activities, methods or tools could help?

Decide what activities, methods or tools I will commit to. How will I use my journal to improve my daily rituals?

Write it down!
Space for your thoughts.

Affirmations for my Mission

Set your Intention

Everything that happens in the universe begins with intention. It is the starting point of every dream.

Decide that you're going to work on your acceptance and gratitude. Be determined to give this journal your best effort.

Repeat this intention daily,

"I am grateful for my sense of gratitude – I know it is the way to joy, peace, and the life of my dreams."

Your intention and determination are the **key to your success**.

30 Day Plan

What are the top 3 goals you'll be working towards in the next **30 days**? Choose **specific goals** that have **measurable results**. Choose goals that **facilitate the journey** to your dream. Choose goals that will be **realistically attainable** BUT also push you out of your comfort zone.

"A goal properly set is halfway reached" - Zig Ziglar

GOAL 1

GOAL
_____
_____
_____

STEPS TO ACHIEVE THIS GOAL
_____
_____
_____
_____
_____
_____
_____

GOAL 2

GOAL
_____
_____
_____

STEPS TO ACHIEVE THIS GOAL
_____
_____
_____
_____
_____
_____
_____

GOAL _____
_____
_____
_____

STEPS TO ACHIEVE THIS GOAL _____
_____
_____
_____
_____
_____
_____
_____

_____
_____
_____
_____
_____
_____
_____
_____
_____
_____
_____
_____
_____

GOAL 3

WHY

What is your driving force behind these goals? What will keep you going when times get tough?

Often when we feel overwhelmed, anxious or unfulfilled, it is because we haven't clearly defined our why!

DATE

EXPRESSING MY *Gratitude*

HEART
_____
_____
_____

HEALTH
_____
_____
_____

MIND
_____
_____
_____

RELATIONSHIPS
_____
_____
_____

MISSION
_____
_____
_____

MANIFESTING MY *Gratitude*

HEART
_____
_____
_____

HEALTH
_____
_____
_____

MIND
_____
_____
_____

RELATIONSHIPS
_____
_____
_____

MISSION
_____
_____
_____

DATE

EXPRESSING MY *Gratitude*

HEART

HEALTH

MIND

RELATIONSHIPS

MISSION

MANIFESTING MY *Gratitude*

HEART

HEALTH

MIND

RELATIONSHIPS

MISSION

DATE

EXPRESSING MY *Gratitude*

HEART

HEALTH

MIND

RELATIONSHIPS

MISSION

MANIFESTING MY *Gratitude*

HEART

HEALTH

MIND

RELATIONSHIPS

MISSION

DATE

EXPRESSING MY *Gratitude*

HEART _____

HEALTH _____

MIND _____

RELATIONSHIPS _____

MISSION _____

MANIFESTING MY *Gratitude*

HEART _____

HEALTH _____

MIND _____

RELATIONSHIPS _____

MISSION _____

DATE

EXPRESSING MY *Gratitude*

- HEART
- HEALTH
- MIND
- RELATIONSHIPS
- MISSION

MANIFESTING MY *Gratitude*

- HEART
- HEALTH
- MIND
- RELATIONSHIPS
- MISSION

DATE _____

EXPRESSING MY *Gratitude*

HEART
_____
_____

HEALTH
_____
_____

MIND
_____
_____

RELATIONSHIPS
_____
_____

MISSION
_____
_____

MANIFESTING MY *Gratitude*

HEART
_____
_____

HEALTH
_____
_____

MIND
_____
_____

RELATIONSHIPS
_____
_____

MISSION
_____
_____

DATE

EXPRESSING MY *Gratitude*

HEART
_____
_____

HEALTH
_____
_____

MIND
_____
_____

RELATIONSHIPS
_____
_____

MISSION
_____
_____

MANIFESTING MY *Gratitude*

HEART
_____
_____

HEALTH
_____
_____

MIND
_____
_____

RELATIONSHIPS
_____
_____

MISSION
_____
_____

DATE

EXPRESSING MY *Gratitude*

HEART
_____
_____

HEALTH
_____
_____

MIND
_____
_____

RELATIONSHIPS
_____
_____

MISSION
_____
_____

MANIFESTING MY *Gratitude*

HEART
_____
_____

HEALTH
_____
_____

MIND
_____
_____

RELATIONSHIPS
_____
_____

MISSION
_____
_____

DATE

EXPRESSING MY *Gratitude*

- **HEART**
- **HEALTH**
- **MIND**
- **RELATIONSHIPS**
- **MISSION**

MANIFESTING MY *Gratitude*

- **HEART**
- **HEALTH**
- **MIND**
- **RELATIONSHIPS**
- **MISSION**

DATE

EXPRESSING MY *Gratitude*

- HEART
- HEALTH
- MIND
- RELATIONSHIPS
- MISSION

MANIFESTING MY *Gratitude*

- HEART
- HEALTH
- MIND
- RELATIONSHIPS
- MISSION

DATE

EXPRESSING MY *Gratitude*

HEART
_____
_____

HEALTH
_____
_____

MIND
_____
_____

RELATIONSHIPS
_____
_____

MISSION
_____
_____

MANIFESTING MY *Gratitude*

HEART
_____
_____

HEALTH
_____
_____

MIND
_____
_____

RELATIONSHIPS
_____
_____

MISSION
_____
_____

DATE

EXPRESSING MY *Gratitude*

HEART

HEALTH

MIND

RELATIONSHIPS

MISSION

MANIFESTING MY *Gratitude*

HEART

HEALTH

MIND

RELATIONSHIPS

MISSION

DATE

EXPRESSING MY *Gratitude*

- **HEART**
- **HEALTH**
- **MIND**
- **RELATIONSHIPS**
- **MISSION**

MANIFESTING MY *Gratitude*

- **HEART**
- **HEALTH**
- **MIND**
- **RELATIONSHIPS**
- **MISSION**

DATE

EXPRESSING MY Gratitude

HEART

HEALTH

MIND

RELATIONSHIPS

MISSION

MANIFESTING MY Gratitude

HEART

HEALTH

MIND

RELATIONSHIPS

MISSION

DATE

EXPRESSING MY Gratitude

HEART
_____
_____

HEALTH
_____
_____

MIND
_____
_____

RELATIONSHIPS
_____
_____

MISSION
_____
_____

MANIFESTING MY Gratitude

HEART
_____
_____

HEALTH
_____
_____

MIND
_____
_____

RELATIONSHIPS
_____
_____

MISSION
_____
_____

DATE

EXPRESSING MY *Gratitude*

HEART
_____
_____

HEALTH
_____
_____

MIND
_____
_____

RELATIONSHIPS
_____
_____

MISSION
_____
_____

MANIFESTING MY *Gratitude*

HEART
_____
_____

HEALTH
_____
_____

MIND
_____
_____

RELATIONSHIPS
_____
_____

MISSION
_____
_____

DATE

EXPRESSING MY *Gratitude*

- HEART
- HEALTH
- MIND
- RELATIONSHIPS
- MISSION

MANIFESTING MY *Gratitude*

- HEART
- HEALTH
- MIND
- RELATIONSHIPS
- MISSION

DATE

EXPRESSING MY *Gratitude*

HEART

HEALTH

MIND

RELATIONSHIPS

MISSION

MANIFESTING MY *Gratitude*

HEART

HEALTH

MIND

RELATIONSHIPS

MISSION

DATE

EXPRESSING MY Gratitude

- HEART
- HEALTH
- MIND
- RELATIONSHIPS
- MISSION

MANIFESTING MY Gratitude

- HEART
- HEALTH
- MIND
- RELATIONSHIPS
- MISSION

DATE

EXPRESSING MY *Gratitude*

HEART
_____
_____

HEALTH
_____
_____

MIND
_____
_____

RELATIONSHIPS
_____
_____

MISSION
_____
_____

MANIFESTING MY *Gratitude*

HEART
_____
_____

HEALTH
_____
_____

MIND
_____
_____

RELATIONSHIPS
_____
_____

MISSION
_____
_____

DATE

EXPRESSING MY *Gratitude*

HEART
_____
_____

HEALTH
_____
_____

MIND
_____
_____

RELATIONSHIPS
_____
_____

MISSION
_____
_____

MANIFESTING MY *Gratitude*

HEART
_____
_____

HEALTH
_____
_____

MIND
_____
_____

RELATIONSHIPS
_____
_____

MISSION
_____
_____

DATE _____

EXPRESSING MY Gratitude

HEART
_____
_____

HEALTH
_____
_____

MIND
_____
_____

RELATIONSHIPS
_____
_____

MISSION
_____
_____

MANIFESTING MY Gratitude

HEART
_____
_____

HEALTH
_____
_____

MIND
_____
_____

RELATIONSHIPS
_____
_____

MISSION
_____
_____

DATE

EXPRESSING MY Gratitude

HEART

HEALTH

MIND

RELATIONSHIPS

MISSION

MANIFESTING MY Gratitude

HEART

HEALTH

MIND

RELATIONSHIPS

MISSION

DATE

EXPRESSING MY *Gratitude*

HEART
_____
_____

HEALTH
_____
_____

MIND
_____
_____

RELATIONSHIPS
_____
_____

MISSION
_____
_____

MANIFESTING MY *Gratitude*

HEART
_____
_____

HEALTH
_____
_____

MIND
_____
_____

RELATIONSHIPS
_____
_____

MISSION
_____
_____

DATE

EXPRESSING MY *Gratitude*

HEART

HEALTH

MIND

RELATIONSHIPS

MISSION

MANIFESTING MY *Gratitude*

HEART

HEALTH

MIND

RELATIONSHIPS

MISSION

DATE

EXPRESSING MY *Gratitude*

HEART
_____
_____

HEALTH
_____
_____

MIND
_____
_____

RELATIONSHIPS
_____
_____

MISSION
_____
_____

MANIFESTING MY *Gratitude*

HEART
_____
_____

HEALTH
_____
_____

MIND
_____
_____

RELATIONSHIPS
_____
_____

MISSION
_____
_____

DATE _____

EXPRESSING MY Gratitude

HEART _____
_____

HEALTH _____
_____

MIND _____
_____

RELATIONSHIPS _____
_____

MISSION _____
_____

MANIFESTING MY Gratitude

HEART _____
_____

HEALTH _____
_____

MIND _____
_____

RELATIONSHIPS _____
_____

MISSION _____
_____

DATE

EXPRESSING MY *Gratitude*

HEART
_____
_____

HEALTH
_____
_____

MIND
_____
_____

RELATIONSHIPS
_____
_____

MISSION
_____
_____

MANIFESTING MY *Gratitude*

HEART
_____
_____

HEALTH
_____
_____

MIND
_____
_____

RELATIONSHIPS
_____
_____

MISSION
_____
_____

DATE

EXPRESSING MY *Gratitude*

- **HEART**
- **HEALTH**
- **MIND**
- **RELATIONSHIPS**
- **MISSION**

MANIFESTING MY *Gratitude*

- **HEART**
- **HEALTH**
- **MIND**
- **RELATIONSHIPS**
- **MISSION**

DATE

EXPRESSING MY *Gratitude*

HEART
_____
_____

HEALTH
_____
_____

MIND
_____
_____

RELATIONSHIPS
_____
_____

MISSION
_____
_____

MANIFESTING MY *Gratitude*

HEART
_____
_____

HEALTH
_____
_____

MIND
_____
_____

RELATIONSHIPS
_____
_____

MISSION
_____
_____

30 Day Plan

What are the top 3 goals you'll be working towards in the next **30 days**? Choose **specific goals** that have **measurable results**. Choose goals that **facilitate the journey** to your dream. Choose goals that will be **realistically attainable** BUT also push you out of your comfort zone.

"A goal properly set is halfway reached" - Zig Ziglar

GOAL 1

GOAL

_____
_____
_____
_____

STEPS TO ACHIEVE THIS GOAL

_____
_____
_____
_____
_____
_____
_____

GOAL 2

GOAL

_____
_____
_____
_____

STEPS TO ACHIEVE THIS GOAL

_____
_____
_____
_____
_____
_____
_____

GOAL

STEPS TO ACHIEVE THIS GOAL

GOAL 3

WHY

What is your driving force behind these goals? What will keep you going when times get tough?

Often when we feel overwhelmed, anxious or unfulfilled, it is because we haven't clearly defined our why!

DATE

EXPRESSING MY *Gratitude*

HEART

HEALTH

MIND

RELATIONSHIPS

MISSION

MANIFESTING MY *Gratitude*

HEART

HEALTH

MIND

RELATIONSHIPS

MISSION

DATE _____

EXPRESSING MY Gratitude

HEART
_____
_____

HEALTH
_____
_____

MIND
_____
_____

RELATIONSHIPS
_____
_____

MISSION
_____
_____

MANIFESTING MY Gratitude

HEART
_____
_____

HEALTH
_____
_____

MIND
_____
_____

RELATIONSHIPS
_____
_____

MISSION
_____
_____

DATE

EXPRESSING MY *Gratitude*

- HEART
- HEALTH
- MIND
- RELATIONSHIPS
- MISSION

MANIFESTING MY *Gratitude*

- HEART
- HEALTH
- MIND
- RELATIONSHIPS
- MISSION

DATE

EXPRESSING MY Gratitude

HEART

HEALTH

MIND

RELATIONSHIPS

MISSION

MANIFESTING MY Gratitude

HEART

HEALTH

MIND

RELATIONSHIPS

MISSION

DATE

EXPRESSING MY *Gratitude*

- HEART
- HEALTH
- MIND
- RELATIONSHIPS
- MISSION

MANIFESTING MY *Gratitude*

- HEART
- HEALTH
- MIND
- RELATIONSHIPS
- MISSION

DATE

EXPRESSING MY Gratitude

HEART

HEALTH

MIND

RELATIONSHIPS

MISSION

MANIFESTING MY Gratitude

HEART

HEALTH

MIND

RELATIONSHIPS

MISSION

DATE

EXPRESSING MY *Gratitude*

HEART

HEALTH

MIND

RELATIONSHIPS

MISSION

MANIFESTING MY *Gratitude*

HEART

HEALTH

MIND

RELATIONSHIPS

MISSION

DATE

EXPRESSING MY Gratitude

HEART
_____
_____

HEALTH
_____
_____

MIND
_____
_____

RELATIONSHIPS
_____
_____

MISSION
_____
_____

MANIFESTING MY Gratitude

HEART
_____
_____

HEALTH
_____
_____

MIND
_____
_____

RELATIONSHIPS
_____
_____

MISSION
_____
_____

DATE

EXPRESSING MY Gratitude

HEART

HEALTH

MIND

RELATIONSHIPS

MISSION

MANIFESTING MY Gratitude

HEART

HEALTH

MIND

RELATIONSHIPS

MISSION

DATE

EXPRESSING MY *Gratitude*

- HEART
- HEALTH
- MIND
- RELATIONSHIPS
- MISSION

MANIFESTING MY *Gratitude*

- HEART
- HEALTH
- MIND
- RELATIONSHIPS
- MISSION

DATE

EXPRESSING MY Gratitude

- **HEART**
- **HEALTH**
- **MIND**
- **RELATIONSHIPS**
- **MISSION**

MANIFESTING MY Gratitude

- **HEART**
- **HEALTH**
- **MIND**
- **RELATIONSHIPS**
- **MISSION**

DATE

EXPRESSING MY Gratitude

HEART
_____
_____

HEALTH
_____
_____

MIND
_____
_____

RELATIONSHIPS
_____
_____

MISSION
_____
_____

MANIFESTING MY Gratitude

HEART
_____
_____

HEALTH
_____
_____

MIND
_____
_____

RELATIONSHIPS
_____
_____

MISSION
_____
_____

DATE

EXPRESSING MY *Gratitude*

- HEART
- HEALTH
- MIND
- RELATIONSHIPS
- MISSION

MANIFESTING MY *Gratitude*

- HEART
- HEALTH
- MIND
- RELATIONSHIPS
- MISSION

DATE

EXPRESSING MY Gratitude

HEART
_____
_____

HEALTH
_____
_____

MIND
_____
_____

RELATIONSHIPS
_____
_____

MISSION
_____
_____

MANIFESTING MY Gratitude

HEART
_____
_____

HEALTH
_____
_____

MIND
_____
_____

RELATIONSHIPS
_____
_____

MISSION
_____
_____

DATE

EXPRESSING MY Gratitude

- **HEART**
- **HEALTH**
- **MIND**
- **RELATIONSHIPS**
- **MISSION**

MANIFESTING MY Gratitude

- **HEART**
- **HEALTH**
- **MIND**
- **RELATIONSHIPS**
- **MISSION**

DATE

EXPRESSING MY *Gratitude*

HEART
_____
_____

HEALTH
_____
_____

MIND
_____
_____

RELATIONSHIPS
_____
_____

MISSION
_____
_____

MANIFESTING MY *Gratitude*

HEART
_____
_____

HEALTH
_____
_____

MIND
_____
_____

RELATIONSHIPS
_____
_____

MISSION
_____
_____

DATE

EXPRESSING MY *Gratitude*

- HEART
- HEALTH
- MIND
- RELATIONSHIPS
- MISSION

MANIFESTING MY *Gratitude*

- HEART
- HEALTH
- MIND
- RELATIONSHIPS
- MISSION

DATE

EXPRESSING MY *Gratitude*

HEART
_____
_____

HEALTH
_____
_____

MIND
_____
_____

RELATIONSHIPS
_____
_____

MISSION
_____
_____

MANIFESTING MY *Gratitude*

HEART
_____
_____

HEALTH
_____
_____

MIND
_____
_____

RELATIONSHIPS
_____
_____

MISSION
_____
_____

DATE _____

EXPRESSING MY *Gratitude*

HEART
_____
_____

HEALTH
_____
_____

MIND
_____
_____

RELATIONSHIPS
_____
_____

MISSION
_____
_____

MANIFESTING MY *Gratitude*

HEART
_____
_____

HEALTH
_____
_____

MIND
_____
_____

RELATIONSHIPS
_____
_____

MISSION
_____
_____

DATE

EXPRESSING MY Gratitude

- HEART
- HEALTH
- MIND
- RELATIONSHIPS
- MISSION

MANIFESTING MY Gratitude

- HEART
- HEALTH
- MIND
- RELATIONSHIPS
- MISSION

DATE

EXPRESSING MY Gratitude

HEART
_____
_____

HEALTH
_____
_____

MIND
_____
_____

RELATIONSHIPS
_____
_____

MISSION
_____
_____

MANIFESTING MY Gratitude

HEART
_____
_____

HEALTH
_____
_____

MIND
_____
_____

RELATIONSHIPS
_____
_____

MISSION
_____
_____

DATE

EXPRESSING MY *Gratitude*

HEART _____

HEALTH _____

MIND _____

RELATIONSHIPS _____

MISSION _____

MANIFESTING MY *Gratitude*

HEART _____

HEALTH _____

MIND _____

RELATIONSHIPS _____

MISSION _____

DATE

EXPRESSING MY Gratitude

HEART
_____
_____
_____

HEALTH
_____
_____
_____

MIND
_____
_____
_____

RELATIONSHIPS
_____
_____
_____

MISSION
_____
_____

MANIFESTING MY Gratitude

HEART
_____
_____
_____

HEALTH
_____
_____
_____

MIND
_____
_____
_____

RELATIONSHIPS
_____
_____
_____

MISSION
_____
_____

DATE

EXPRESSING MY Gratitude

HEART
_____
_____

HEALTH
_____
_____

MIND
_____
_____

RELATIONSHIPS
_____
_____

MISSION
_____
_____

MANIFESTING MY Gratitude

HEART
_____
_____

HEALTH
_____
_____

MIND
_____
_____

RELATIONSHIPS
_____
_____

MISSION
_____
_____

DATE

EXPRESSING MY Gratitude

- **HEART**
- **HEALTH**
- **MIND**
- **RELATIONSHIPS**
- **MISSION**

MANIFESTING MY Gratitude

- **HEART**
- **HEALTH**
- **MIND**
- **RELATIONSHIPS**
- **MISSION**

DATE

EXPRESSING MY Gratitude

- HEART
- HEALTH
- MIND
- RELATIONSHIPS
- MISSION

MANIFESTING MY Gratitude

- HEART
- HEALTH
- MIND
- RELATIONSHIPS
- MISSION

DATE

EXPRESSING MY *Gratitude*

HEART
_____
_____

HEALTH
_____
_____

MIND
_____
_____

RELATIONSHIPS
_____
_____

MISSION
_____
_____

MANIFESTING MY *Gratitude*

HEART
_____
_____

HEALTH
_____
_____

MIND
_____
_____

RELATIONSHIPS
_____
_____

MISSION
_____
_____

DATE _____

EXPRESSING MY *Gratitude*

HEART
_____
_____

HEALTH
_____
_____

MIND
_____
_____

RELATIONSHIPS
_____
_____

MISSION
_____
_____

MANIFESTING MY *Gratitude*

HEART
_____
_____

HEALTH
_____
_____

MIND
_____
_____

RELATIONSHIPS
_____
_____

MISSION
_____
_____

DATE

EXPRESSING MY *Gratitude*

- HEART
- HEALTH
- MIND
- RELATIONSHIPS
- MISSION

MANIFESTING MY *Gratitude*

- HEART
- HEALTH
- MIND
- RELATIONSHIPS
- MISSION

DATE

EXPRESSING MY *Gratitude*

HEART
_____
_____

HEALTH
_____
_____

MIND
_____
_____

RELATIONSHIPS
_____
_____

MISSION
_____
_____

MANIFESTING MY *Gratitude*

HEART
_____
_____

HEALTH
_____
_____

MIND
_____
_____

RELATIONSHIPS
_____
_____

MISSION
_____
_____

30 Day Plan

What are the top 3 goals you'll be working towards in the next **30 days**? Choose **specific goals** that have **measurable results**. Choose goals that **facilitate the journey** to your dream. Choose goals that will be **realistically attainable** BUT also push you out of your comfort zone.

"A goal properly set is halfway reached" - Zig Ziglar

GOAL 1

GOAL
_____
_____
_____
_____

STEPS TO ACHIEVE THIS GOAL
_____
_____
_____
_____
_____
_____
_____

GOAL 2

GOAL
_____
_____
_____
_____

STEPS TO ACHIEVE THIS GOAL
_____
_____
_____
_____
_____
_____
_____

GOAL

STEPS TO ACHIEVE THIS GOAL

GOAL 3

WHY

What is your driving force behind these goals? What will keep you going when times get tough?

Often when we feel overwhelmed, anxious or unfulfilled, it is because we haven't clearly defined our why!

DATE

EXPRESSING MY *Gratitude*

- **HEART**
- **HEALTH**
- **MIND**
- **RELATIONSHIPS**
- **MISSION**

MANIFESTING MY *Gratitude*

- **HEART**
- **HEALTH**
- **MIND**
- **RELATIONSHIPS**
- **MISSION**

DATE

EXPRESSING MY *Gratitude*

- **HEART**
- **HEALTH**
- **MIND**
- **RELATIONSHIPS**
- **MISSION**

MANIFESTING MY *Gratitude*

- **HEART**
- **HEALTH**
- **MIND**
- **RELATIONSHIPS**
- **MISSION**

DATE

EXPRESSING MY *Gratitude*

HEART
_____
_____
_____

HEALTH
_____
_____
_____

MIND
_____
_____
_____

RELATIONSHIPS
_____
_____
_____

MISSION
_____
_____
_____

MANIFESTING MY *Gratitude*

HEART
_____
_____
_____

HEALTH
_____
_____
_____

MIND
_____
_____
_____

RELATIONSHIPS
_____
_____
_____

MISSION
_____
_____
_____

DATE

EXPRESSING MY Gratitude

HEART
_____
_____

HEALTH
_____
_____

MIND
_____
_____

RELATIONSHIPS
_____
_____

MISSION
_____
_____

MANIFESTING MY Gratitude

HEART
_____
_____

HEALTH
_____
_____

MIND
_____
_____

RELATIONSHIPS
_____
_____

MISSION
_____
_____

DATE

EXPRESSING MY *Gratitude*

HEART

HEALTH

MIND

RELATIONSHIPS

MISSION

MANIFESTING MY *Gratitude*

HEART

HEALTH

MIND

RELATIONSHIPS

MISSION

DATE _____

EXPRESSING MY Gratitude

HEART
_____
_____

HEALTH
_____
_____

MIND
_____
_____

RELATIONSHIPS
_____
_____

MISSION
_____
_____

MANIFESTING MY Gratitude

HEART
_____
_____

HEALTH
_____
_____

MIND
_____
_____

RELATIONSHIPS
_____
_____

MISSION
_____
_____

DATE

EXPRESSING MY *Gratitude*

- **HEART**
- **HEALTH**
- **MIND**
- **RELATIONSHIPS**
- **MISSION**

MANIFESTING MY *Gratitude*

- **HEART**
- **HEALTH**
- **MIND**
- **RELATIONSHIPS**
- **MISSION**

DATE

EXPRESSING MY *Gratitude*

- HEART
- HEALTH
- MIND
- RELATIONSHIPS
- MISSION

MANIFESTING MY *Gratitude*

- HEART
- HEALTH
- MIND
- RELATIONSHIPS
- MISSION

DATE

EXPRESSING MY *Gratitude*

HEART
_____
_____

HEALTH
_____
_____

MIND
_____
_____

RELATIONSHIPS
_____
_____

MISSION
_____
_____

MANIFESTING MY *Gratitude*

HEART
_____
_____

HEALTH
_____
_____

MIND
_____
_____

RELATIONSHIPS
_____
_____

MISSION
_____
_____

DATE

EXPRESSING MY Gratitude

HEART _____

HEALTH _____

MIND _____

RELATIONSHIPS _____

MISSION _____

MANIFESTING MY Gratitude

HEART _____

HEALTH _____

MIND _____

RELATIONSHIPS _____

MISSION _____

DATE

EXPRESSING MY *Gratitude*

- **HEART**
- **HEALTH**
- **MIND**
- **RELATIONSHIPS**
- **MISSION**

MANIFESTING MY *Gratitude*

- **HEART**
- **HEALTH**
- **MIND**
- **RELATIONSHIPS**
- **MISSION**

DATE

EXPRESSING MY *Gratitude*

HEART

HEALTH

MIND

RELATIONSHIPS

MISSION

MANIFESTING MY *Gratitude*

HEART

HEALTH

MIND

RELATIONSHIPS

MISSION

DATE

EXPRESSING MY *Gratitude*

HEART

HEALTH

MIND

RELATIONSHIPS

MISSION

MANIFESTING MY *Gratitude*

HEART

HEALTH

MIND

RELATIONSHIPS

MISSION

DATE _____

EXPRESSING MY *Gratitude*

HEART _____

HEALTH _____

MIND _____

RELATIONSHIPS _____

MISSION _____

MANIFESTING MY *Gratitude*

HEART _____

HEALTH _____

MIND _____

RELATIONSHIPS _____

MISSION _____

DATE

EXPRESSING MY *Gratitude*

HEART
_____
_____

HEALTH
_____
_____

MIND
_____
_____

RELATIONSHIPS
_____
_____

MISSION
_____
_____

MANIFESTING MY *Gratitude*

HEART
_____
_____

HEALTH
_____
_____

MIND
_____
_____

RELATIONSHIPS
_____
_____

MISSION
_____
_____

DATE

EXPRESSING MY *Gratitude*

HEART
_____
_____

HEALTH
_____
_____

MIND
_____
_____

RELATIONSHIPS
_____
_____

MISSION
_____
_____

MANIFESTING MY *Gratitude*

HEART
_____
_____

HEALTH
_____
_____

MIND
_____
_____

RELATIONSHIPS
_____
_____

MISSION
_____
_____

DATE _____

EXPRESSING MY Gratitude

HEART
_____
_____

HEALTH
_____
_____

MIND
_____
_____

RELATIONSHIPS
_____
_____

MISSION
_____
_____

MANIFESTING MY Gratitude

HEART
_____
_____

HEALTH
_____
_____

MIND
_____
_____

RELATIONSHIPS
_____
_____

MISSION
_____
_____

DATE _____

EXPRESSING MY *Gratitude*

HEART
_____
_____

HEALTH
_____
_____

MIND
_____
_____

RELATIONSHIPS
_____
_____

MISSION
_____
_____

MANIFESTING MY *Gratitude*

HEART
_____
_____

HEALTH
_____
_____

MIND
_____
_____

RELATIONSHIPS
_____
_____

MISSION
_____
_____

DATE

EXPRESSING MY *Gratitude*

HEART

HEALTH

MIND

RELATIONSHIPS

MISSION

MANIFESTING MY *Gratitude*

HEART

HEALTH

MIND

RELATIONSHIPS

MISSION

DATE _____

EXPRESSING MY *Gratitude*

HEART
_____
_____

HEALTH
_____
_____

MIND
_____
_____

RELATIONSHIPS
_____
_____

MISSION
_____
_____

MANIFESTING MY *Gratitude*

HEART
_____
_____

HEALTH
_____
_____

MIND
_____
_____

RELATIONSHIPS
_____
_____

MISSION
_____
_____

DATE

EXPRESSING MY *Gratitude*

- HEART
- HEALTH
- MIND
- RELATIONSHIPS
- MISSION

MANIFESTING MY *Gratitude*

- HEART
- HEALTH
- MIND
- RELATIONSHIPS
- MISSION

DATE

EXPRESSING MY *Gratitude*

HEART
_____
_____

HEALTH
_____
_____

MIND
_____
_____

RELATIONSHIPS
_____
_____

MISSION
_____
_____

MANIFESTING MY *Gratitude*

HEART
_____
_____

HEALTH
_____
_____

MIND
_____
_____

RELATIONSHIPS
_____
_____

MISSION
_____
_____

DATE

EXPRESSING MY *Gratitude*

- HEART _____
- HEALTH _____
- MIND _____
- RELATIONSHIPS _____
- MISSION _____

MANIFESTING MY *Gratitude*

- HEART _____
- HEALTH _____
- MIND _____
- RELATIONSHIPS _____
- MISSION _____

DATE

EXPRESSING MY *Gratitude*

HEART

HEALTH

MIND

RELATIONSHIPS

MISSION

MANIFESTING MY *Gratitude*

HEART

HEALTH

MIND

RELATIONSHIPS

MISSION

DATE

EXPRESSING MY *Gratitude*

HEART

HEALTH

MIND

RELATIONSHIPS

MISSION

MANIFESTING MY *Gratitude*

HEART

HEALTH

MIND

RELATIONSHIPS

MISSION

DATE

EXPRESSING MY Gratitude

HEART
_____
_____

HEALTH
_____
_____

MIND
_____
_____

RELATIONSHIPS
_____
_____

MISSION
_____
_____

MANIFESTING MY Gratitude

HEART
_____
_____

HEALTH
_____
_____

MIND
_____
_____

RELATIONSHIPS
_____
_____

MISSION
_____
_____

DATE

EXPRESSING MY *Gratitude*

- HEART
- HEALTH
- MIND
- RELATIONSHIPS
- MISSION

MANIFESTING MY *Gratitude*

- HEART
- HEALTH
- MIND
- RELATIONSHIPS
- MISSION

DATE

EXPRESSING MY Gratitude

HEART _____

HEALTH _____

MIND _____

RELATIONSHIPS _____

MISSION _____

MANIFESTING MY Gratitude

HEART _____

HEALTH _____

MIND _____

RELATIONSHIPS _____

MISSION _____

DATE

EXPRESSING MY *Gratitude*

- **HEART**
- **HEALTH**
- **MIND**
- **RELATIONSHIPS**
- **MISSION**

MANIFESTING MY *Gratitude*

- **HEART**
- **HEALTH**
- **MIND**
- **RELATIONSHIPS**
- **MISSION**

DATE

EXPRESSING MY *Gratitude*

HEART
_____
_____

HEALTH
_____
_____

MIND
_____
_____

RELATIONSHIPS
_____
_____

MISSION
_____
_____

MANIFESTING MY *Gratitude*

HEART
_____
_____

HEALTH
_____
_____

MIND
_____
_____

RELATIONSHIPS
_____
_____

MISSION
_____
_____

SPECIAL BONUS
FREE BOOKS

FREE Workbook to help you understand the journaling process used in this book.

FREE 30 Days to Greater Self Love Program to follow whilst journaling.

Get FREE unlimited access to these AND all of my new books by joining our fan base!

SCAN WITH YOUR CAMERA OR GO TO
bit.ly/GuidedJournalingWorkbook

Journals in the **Guided Journaling** Series...

Journaling for a Balanced Life with a **Health** focus

Journaling for a Balanced Life with a **Life Mission** focus

Journaling for a Balanced Life with a focus on the **Heart**

Journaling for a Balanced Life with a **Gratitude** & **Manifest** focus

We have a selection of *journals* available worldwide as print or ebook at Amazon, Booktopia, Barnes & Noble and all good bookstores.
Also available in Australia from **turtlepublishing.com.au**